To Dee~
Keep love and
Joy in your life!

Karolyn Grimes
"Zuzu"

Zuzu's Wonderful Life
in the Movies

By
Christopher Brunell

12-14-00

This book is dedicated to my daughter Jennifer.
She brings me much joy and makes my life...*Wonderful*.

Acknowledgments

The author would like to express his thanks to the following people who helped in the preparation of this book: Marge Bakalar, Clay Eals, John Mencl, Mike Downs and Lorena Cohn.

Special thanks to the Jimmy Stewart Estate for all their good wishes and support.

A heartfelt thanks to Karolyn Grimes, who gave me the opportunity to sift through her memories to make this book a reality.

Contents

Section I

Section II

Filmography—Section III
Karolyn and Her Movies

Section IV

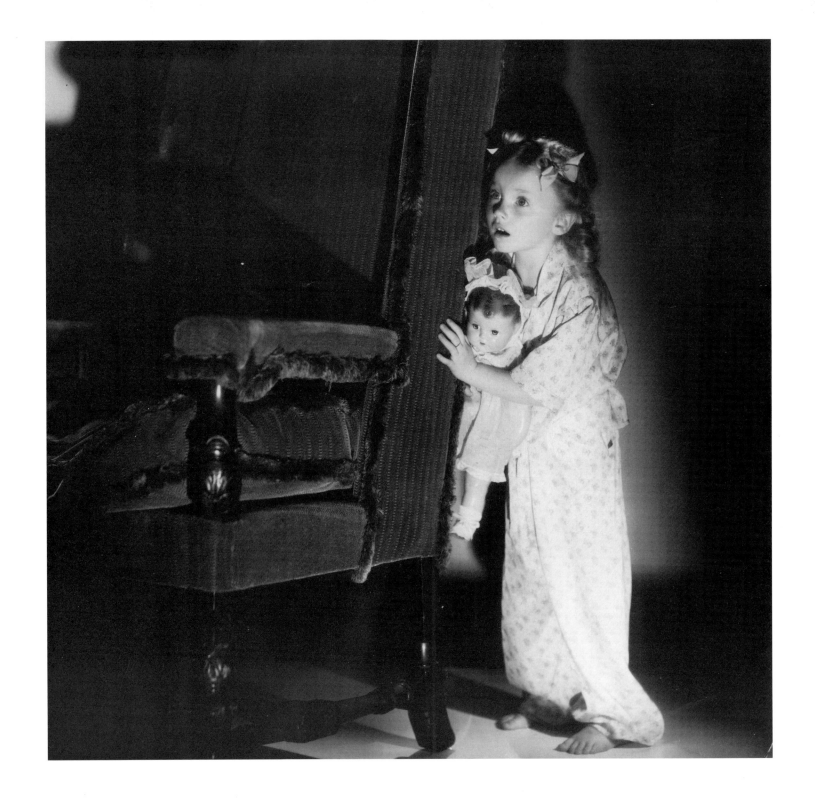

About the Author

Christopher Brunell

Chris Brunell is well acquainted with Karolyn Grimes and her career. In travels with Karolyn, he has been amazed at the growing interest in her movie career and in particular *It's a Wonderful Life.* Chris decided to put this book together to give something to those interested in looking into the golden era of movies as well as the film career of Karolyn Grimes. He is a licensed clinical psychologist and a licensed marriage and family therapist.

Introduction

I met Karolyn Grimes while attending a conference for which she was the keynote speaker. It was the first time she had spoken in public about her personal life. As a Psychologist, I recognized that she was conquering an emotional hurdle. I wanted to meet her. In getting to know each other, we discovered that we shared many of the same values and goals. Karolyn doesn't believe in coincidences. She thinks things happen for a reason.

I was deeply impressed with the profound effect Karolyn had on those who wanted to meet Zuzu. Her inviting smile instantly warmed their hearts. I could see how meeting this remarkable woman was an experience that meant so much. She is someone who, through trials and challenges, has been an inspiration and hope for others. Her capacity for warmth and compassion goes beyond what you would expect. Karolyn is one and the same as Zuzu. She lives the premise from her signature movie, that "Each man's life touches another."

—Christopher Brunell

Moments in Time

By John Mencl, President of the Zuzu Society

Most people don't remember every scene in an entire film, even if it is one of their favorites. What they remember are moments in the film. Something about these moments so touched the heart that the scene is forever remembered. Karolyn Grimes was right in the middle of two such moments, both of which were in my favorite film, *It's A Wonderful Life.*

The first moment is when a frustrated and frantic George Bailey goes upstairs to check on Zuzu who is in bed. George feels like his world is falling apart around him. He thinks that all the times he gave up his own personal ambitions to "do the right thing, and answer the call of duty to help others" were meaningless.

Because of the shortfall at the building and loan he is about to bring bankruptcy and dishonor upon his family. Yet, despite his desperate feelings of despair, he is able to once more put others first and give Zuzu his full attention. He unselfishly gives Zuzu the tenderness, compassion, and love she needed when she was sick in bed with a fever. Then, to top it all, he has the presence of mind to cleverly hide the petals in his watch pocket making Zuzu think he actually pasted some fallen petals back onto the flower so she would stop worrying about it and get the sleep she needed. In my opinion

Karolyn shares a moment with John and his wife Ruth at an appearance at Donna Reed's hometown in Iowa.

this is the most tender scene between a father and daughter ever filmed. These same throwaway Zuzu's petals, of course, later turn out to worth much more to George than the missing $8,000 that started all of his problems.

The other moment in time I will always remember (along with about 100 million of my closest friends!) is when Zuzu says in the closing scene of the film after someone bumps the Christmas tree and a bell shakes and rings, "Look daddy! 'Teacher says, every time a bell rings an angel gets his wings!'" How many of you have noticed, however, that after Jimmy, Donna, and Zuzu sing the first few words of *Auld Lang Syne*, it appears that they don't know the rest of the lyrics? But what 6 year old child and middle age man does? That's one of the reasons the scene seems real to me. The whole closing scene emotionally gets to me every time.

It has been a pleasure for me to serve as President of the Zuzu Society and be present at some of Karolyn's personal appearances around the country. *Fans of It's a Wonderful Life* are genuinely excited and grateful to be able to share a moment in time with the little girl who played Zuzu in this most memorable film.

Karolyn poses
for a publicity
photo at the
tender age of 5.
This is one of
the photos that
was included in
her portfolio
when she was
interviewed
for a part.

Karolyn's Early Years

Who has not heard the line, "Look, daddy, teacher says, 'Every time a bell rings, an angel get his wings ?'" Karolyn Grimes, in 1946 who spoke that line in the movie, has lived a life full of challenges, and she keeps learning that the way to live a "wonderful life" is to embrace the values of family, friends and life's greatest gift.

Karolyn is best remembered as Zuzu, when she delivered this line as a child in the arms of Jimmy Stewart. This magical moment appeared at the end of the movie *It's a Wonderful Life*. It conjures up feelings of family togetherness and values that help us to reflect on what really is important in our lives today.

Karolyn, as Zuzu, has just uttered the line, "Look daddy, teacher says, 'Every time a bell rings an angel gets his wings.'"

Americans have grown up with Zuzu in their homes each year at Christmas. She represents everything that is innocent and pure in their hearts—the youthful hope of what can be, the possibilities for the future.

Karolyn recognizes this and respects how this interplays with the perceived fantasy or projection of whom she represents. For some, it's like meeting Santa Claus for the very first time. It brings a sense of awe and wonderment.

"Everywhere I go, people share their stories with me," Karolyn says. "It's a privilege being part of their lives."

She has an effervescent and genuine personality. She's someone who loves to meet people; she has never met a stranger. But Karolyn is no stranger to the limelight. At an early age she was groomed to be in front of people.

Growing up in Hollywood, Karolyn got her start on the silver screen as a preschooler and eventually appeared in 16 movies with Cary Grant, John Wayne, Bing Crosby and many other stars. She vividly recalls her movie interview for the part of Zuzu.

"There were lots of little girls at the interview," she says. "You've heard of the typical stage mother. One of them spilled coffee on my dress 'by accident.' It might have upset other little girls to go into the interview with a soiled dress, but it gave me something to talk about. I think it landed me the part."

Karolyn's mother was born Martha Octavia Motley. She was raised in the flatlands of Missouri. She is probably best described as a country girl only because she lived in the country. Always dreaming of escaping her rustic life as a schoolteacher, she got her wish when she married a handsome and bright young man named Ernest LaVan Grimes.

The Depression was wreaking havoc on the Midwest,

The wedding photo of Karolyn's parents, Martha and LaVan Grimes

LaVan and Martha Grimes cuddle with their first and only child in the tiny living room of their house on West Norton Ave.

and her father and mother decided to gamble on a better future by moving to the West Coast. The destination was Hollywood, Calif.

While America was in the throes of World War II, Karolyn's parents were struggling like everyone else to keep financially stable. In those days, there was no such thing as credit cards; everyone paid in cash. Soon, there would be rationing and many changes that would make survival even more of a challenge.

Karolyn's mother was afraid that LaVan would be drafted. She worried that she couldn't survive on Army pay, and she didn't want to work for pay herself. So she decided to put Karolyn to work.

She had a friend who had a child in the movie business, and that child had an agent. Her mother took Karolyn to see the agent, Lola Moore, who at that time was well-known for her stable of children actors. Lola took Karolyn as a client, and soon she started getting parts. The irony is that on the day Karolyn's father was to leave for the Army, the war ended. Her father

Karolyn at the age of one year.

never had to leave.

For her interviews for movie parts, Karolyn would have her portfolio with lots of pictures that demonstrated the emotions she could display. Thus she entered the casting office with confidence that she could do whatever they asked of her.

It seemed at that time that the same bunch of little girls were always trying out for each role. They played together in the outside office before each was whisked to the main office for an interview with the casting director, director, producer and whoever else would be involved. Lana Wood, Carol Nugent, GiGi Perreau and other little starlets became a regular part of Karolyn's life.

Karolyn age 4, already sporting her familiar curly locks, performed in her first play, "Mozart."

Karolyn's mother did her best to make Karolyn cute and darling. Karolyn is sure that is why she made up her hair in braids and put bun curls on top of her head. They became her trademark.

Movie studio lots were magical for Karolyn. So many things that looked real *really* were not. Many houses and trees were not real at all. Everything was just a façade.

"The studio sets had a certain

The camera loved Karolyn, and she was a veteran at posing at the age of 4.

smell that I came to love and still do to this day," she says. "Perhaps it was a combination of paint, storage and lights. There were always the huge cables and switch boxes to climb around and not get tangled in. Then there were the lights, hundreds of them everywhere. And, of course, there was the big red light over the door inside and out. This light would go on when they were shooting a scene. We could not go in if the light was on. If the light was shining on the inside of the set, we could not make any noise. So we were guided by the light, so to speak."

Being a child actor was a double-edged sword. There were lots of perks, such as meeting movie stars and living in a magical world of make-believe.

But Karolyn had to pay her dues to participate in this special life. She spent hours under hot lights in front of a camera for publicity shots. Posing and smiling became a staple of her everyday life.

Karolyn had magic early on and learned how to capture hearts.

"Holding still and smiling, following all the directions that people gave me was mind-boggling," she says. "However, I must admit that being the center of everyone's attention wasn't all that bad. It became quite natural and today I still enjoy the limelight."

Part of the process was the array of costumes. "I loved to go to the Western Costume Company to get fitted for wardrobe," Karolyn says. "I could play dress-up all day long. It was a huge building, with many floors of period clothing. I certainly got to wear a lot of nightgowns and robes because it seemed as if I was always in bed."

In the year after World War II, servicemen came home after fighting wars against two formidable countries, both well-armed and on opposite sides of the globe. It had been a long, destructive and costly war. It finally came to a close in the Pacific after two atomic bombs were dropped on the Japanese homeland. Like many of the servicemen who fought the war, America—and the whole world—had changed.

Life took a fateful turn in 1946 for Karolyn as well. With four movies under her belt at the age of 6, Karolyn interviewed and was chosen for the part of Zuzu in the now-classic film *It's a Wonderful Life*. Frank Capra produced the movie through his newly formed Liberty Films. His sentimental story about a man and his guardian angel was full of nostalgia for American small-town life, reflecting the yearning of many people for a time and place before the war, a time which was much less complicated.

The movie was vintage Capra, a populist fantasy of an idealized, American, communal coziness. The movie had respectable success in late 1940s movie houses, but three decades later skyrocketed onto the small screen ultimately becoming a Christmas time TV staple. At the time, however, no one had any idea that this film would come to have an indelible impact on American film history.

Karolyn's charming smile captures the camera as she poses for a publicity photo at age 3 years.

During the filming, Capra displayed his family values and the compassion for life that made him a creative and talented man. Whenever he gave Karolyn directions, he got down on his knees and talked to her at eye level, telling her where he wanted her to look or how to act.

Eight years after the filming of *It's a Wonderful Life*, Karolyn again worked with Thomas Mitchell (Uncle Billy) in a TV program, *Good of his Soul*. He appeared exactly the same to her, as if he had never aged.

Karolyn surrounded by her Christmas gifts. Christmas 1946, the year she played Zuzu.

Karolyn never saw Henry Travers (Clarence) again, but she feels that his portrayal as an angel was perfect casting. They shared a line in this film that has become a part of film history: "Every time a bell rings, an angel gets his wings." Their words are truly immortal.

"It may seem strange to some people," Karolyn says, "but I feel as if Clarence and George Bailey are both watching over me today."

While Karolyn's Hollywood career went into high gear after *It's a Wonderful Life*, events began to take place in her home life that would affect her forever.

First came her mother's early-onset Alzheimer's disease. It advanced slowly, imperceptibly and began to creep into the Grimes' lives.

Despite Karolyn's busy schedule of six feature-length films and one short subject from early 1947 to early 1948, her movie days started to decline. She isn't sure if it was her mother's condition or the beginning of the industry's huge adjustment to the new invention called television.

Some people thought TV spelled permanent doom to the movies. Indeed it did trigger a pause and an insecurity that was hard to dispel. There was a definite decrease in the production of films. Karolyn overheard people say that while 50 films usually were in production at any one time, the number had dwindled to 18.

Karolyn's film appearances dwindled, too, as the 20th century hit its halfway point. And with the onset of TV, Karolyn's acting moved into the new medium. She was in at least one *Ford Theater* and *Fireside Theater* production and a Sugar Smacks commercial starring George Reeves, TV's *Superman*.

No supernatural force could save her mother, however. After six long years, she died. Although it was expected, it was devastating.

A visit with Santa Claus

Often the pose – as with Karolyn's china-doll look – did the trick.

Karolyn dancing at an Easter program

And everything changed. Now it was just Karolyn and her father, starting a new way of life.

By this time, Karolyn had started high school. She was the concert mistress in her orchestra in elementary school and in junior high school. Because she was the head violinist, it was her responsibility to lead the orchestra in tuning and getting ready for the conductor. Music had been instilled in her life at age 5 by her mother, who made sure Karolyn had piano, violin and voice lessons throughout her youth. After losing her mother, Karolyn found comfort in continuing to participate in the practices that she and her mother had shared.

Then came another shock. One year after the death of her mother, Karolyn's father was killed in an automobile accident. At age 15, Karolyn became an orphan and a ward of the court.

Karolyn says she has no regrets that she was shipped off to live with strict relatives in Missouri. "It saved me," she says. She went from a Los Angeles High School class of 900 to the tiny town of Osceola, Missouri with a total of 800 residents.

Karolyn never returned to Hollywood to live. She claimed that in the Midwest she had found her own Bedford Falls. She made the choice to get an education and became a medical technologist. She married her high school sweetheart. They had two daughters. Unfortunately, her marriage was not destined to remain intact, and after five years of marriage, they were divorced. Shortly after, he was killed in a hunting accident. Even though they were no longer married, his loss was an emotional blow.

A few years later, Karolyn married again. Her new husband had three children, so with her two, they started their marriage with five. Eventually they added two more. After spending 25 years raising children, she faced another challenge when her husband was diagnosed with and died of cancer.

Perhaps the most profound challenge of all was the suicide of her son John, at age 18. The emotional trauma took its toll on Karolyn, but with time and an enormous capability for survival, Karolyn started healing. Eventually, she was

Karolyn performs at a recital. She started playing the violin at the age of 6.

Achieving the position as Concert Mistress of the Burnside Elementary School, Karolyn continued her interest in music.

Karolyn cavorts with her dog named Bing

Karolyn, age 9, and her dog Cisco in a park

able to speak publicly about how she had overcome her debilitating grief.

As a wife and mother, Karolyn had long since forgotten her Hollywood days. All her memorabilia was in boxes in the basement. Every once in a while, when her children were young, they took a movie still to school for show-and-tell, but for the most part, all that nostalgia lay untouched. Then one day Karolyn got a telephone call from a local newspaper. The reporter wanted to know if Karolyn was the real Zuzu. With that, the new, inestimably powerful and positive focus of her later life had begun.

By the early 1980s, as a natural outgrowth of its newfound popularity, *It's a Wonderful Life* had become a grassroots cult film. People wanting to share with loved ones the movie's themes of hope, friendship, family and the worth of every human being started giving *It's a Wonderful Life* parties. The trend was legitimized further by lengthy analyses in the media, including *The New Yorker* and *The Wall Street Journal*.

After an absence of some 40 years, with the media coverage came the return of fan mail. Karolyn started receiving fan letters from people who wanted to know what had happened to Zuzu.

Because Karolyn never was shy she received requests for interviews, tackling them with relish. Her identity was transforming. People were beginning to associate this wife and mother with Zuzu Bailey, a symbol of the goodness that each life can create.

A woman with a local radio show wanted Karolyn to come on for an interview. After the show, she said, "I have to share something with you." She told Karolyn that *It's a Wonderful Life* was her brother's favorite movie. He had been in the Navy, when that year his plane had gone down and he was killed. When she got the telephone call notifying her of the accident, she hung up the telephone, walked over and picked up a bell and rang it. She said, "I couldn't do anything, but by ringing that bell I felt like I was doing ... something." She and Karolyn had a good cry, but the seeds were planted, and Karolyn realized that the movie was going to grow.

Some of Karolyn's fans got together in Chicago, forming a fan club called The Zuzu Society. They "gave" the club to her for Christmas. It started with 19 members, but after she began publishing a newsletter, the number grew. People started to send her angels, and the fan mail continued to grow.

Today, Karolyn can be found making personal appearances all over the world.

Karolyn as she appeared for a photo shoot when she was 14 years old.

Filmography

Karolyn and Her Movies

From 1944 through 1952 Karolyn appeared in over 16 movies that are chronicled in this book. On the following pages Karolyn recounts some of her experiences about each of these films. This was a golden age in cinema and Karolyn had the good fortune to be associated with some of the greatest stars in Hollywood film history.

Karolyn thinks that she had parts in several other films. She was too young to remember movie names. Before the age of computers, that kind of information sometimes did not make it into the records. Orphaned at the age of 15, there was no one to document these facts.

Most of the stars who appear in this book have already "gotten their wings." They worked hard, won the respect of millions, and had the ability to make a character come alive on the screen. She knew them not only as great actors but as friends

That Night With You

Produced By: Universal
Director: William A. Seiter
Release date: In the Fall of 1945
84 minutes

Stars: Franchot Tone, Susanna Foster, David Bruce, Buster Keaton

Karolyn's role: [Filmed June 30 and July 2-3, 1945] She plays one of six orphans. She has only two spoken lines, but they are more than throwaways.

Comment: Light musical vehicle for soprano Foster, starring as an ambitious singer who convinces a big producer that she's his long-lost daughter so he'll support her career. Tone is suave, and Foster is appealing. Bruce is just right as the romantic diner owner whose vision of getting married and having six kids. All of this flies in the face of Foster's dreams of stardom. The "father-daughter" relationship between Tone and Foster is curiously risqué for its time.

Karolyn's Comments: "The first role that I remember working on was that of a little orphan girl in the movie, *That Night With You*. I didn't know that, in a few years, being an orphan would be a reality for me. I was four years old, and for my part was to break an ornament that was hanging on a Christmas tree.

One of my favorite scenes was when I lay in Suzanna Foster's arms while she sang me a lullaby. I was supposed to act as if I was asleep. It was hard not to look at her because she was so beautiful. This special moment will always remain in my heart."

Trivia: Playing the ever-frustrated maid in Tone's apartment, as she escorts Karolyn and the other orphans into the presence of Tone's would-be wife Susanna Foster, is the young Irene Ryan, best known 20 years later as Granny in TV's *Beverly Hillbillies*.

Photo left: Susanna Foster, well known for her lilting soprano voice, poses for a publicity photo with a score of music in the background.

Karolyn, second from the left, plays one of a group of orphans from the movie, *That Night With You*. Standing in the background is Irene Ryan.

From left to right: Franchot Tone, Susanna Foster, David Bruce, and Louise Allbritton, from the movie, *That Night With You*.

Pardon My Past

Produced By: Columbia
Director: Leslie Fenton
Release date: February 8, 1946
88 Minutes, Black and White

Stars: Fred MacMurray, Marguerite Chapman, Akim Tamiroff, Rita Johnson, Harry Davenport, William Demerest

Karolyn's role: [Filmed May 1945] Eighth in the credits, she plays Stephani, the daughter of one of the MacMurray characters.

Comment: Ex-soldier is mistaken for a wealthy playboy who owes money to some gamblers. It is a delightful comedy-drama, smoothly done and entertaining. The plot of mistaken identity works well here, largely because of the clever script. But also because of MacMurray's ability to carve two characters who are different from each other, though not so different as to be unbelievable as identical twins. It's also easy to see why Karolyn drew favorable press attention. Here is a performance quite demanding for a child not yet 5 years old.

Karolyn's Comments: "Fred MacMurray, playing twins, was my father as well as my uncle. One memory always makes me chuckle. We were on location at a Beverly Hills mansion to film an outside scene. In the backyard where we were filming, I remember that there was a remarkable freestanding building just sitting in the yard. It was beautifully decorated inside like a Sultan's Palace. I was astonished to find out that this palace was a giant bathroom! This bathroom was four times the size of my ownhouse. It was then that I knew there were small and large bathrooms in this world."

Trivia: It's fun to see MacMurray's easy rapport with sidekick Demerest as the two teamed up similarly in the 1960's on TV's *My Three Sons*.

Photo left: Dressing room photo showing Karolyn with the dress she will be wearing for some publicity shoots.

4

This promotional photo cleverly uses Karolyn to convey the screwball atmosphere of *Pardon My Past*. In the farce, Rita Johnson (left) and Fred MacMurray (playing Francis Pemberton), are Karolyn's parents. MacMurray also plays Eddie York, who doesn't know he is Pemberton's twin. Circumstances prompt York to impersonate Pemberton and fall in love with Karolyn's "Aunt Joan" (Marguerite Chapman, right).

In this scene,
Fred MacMurray (Eddie)
meets Karolyn for the first time as
Marguerite Chapman looks on.

Karolyn, in preparation for a scene from *Pardon My Past*, gets a make-up job and a hair work over.

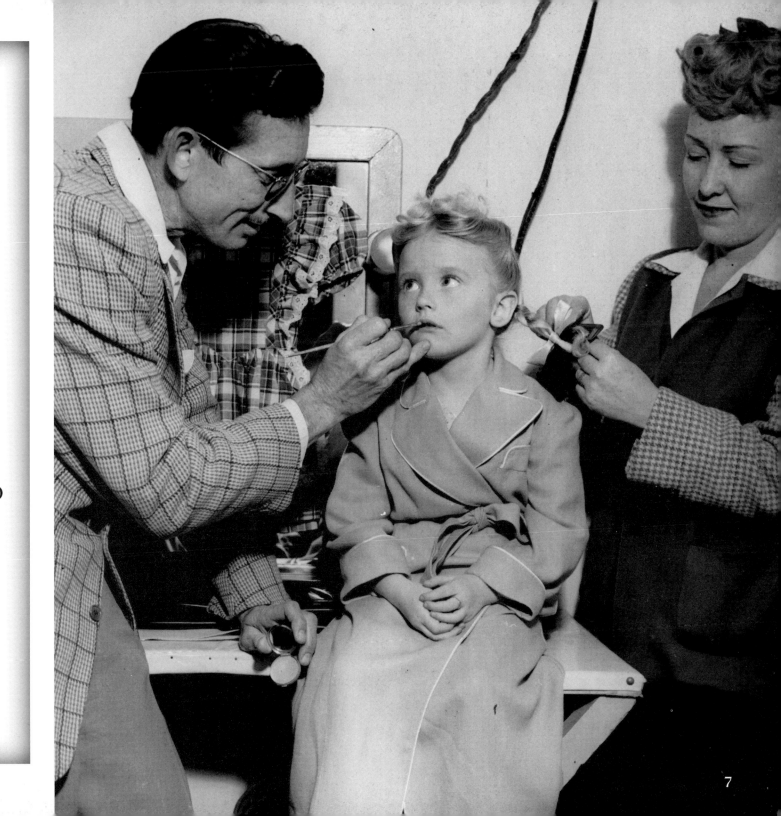

(Left) MacMurray comes along at the right time to assist Karolyn off camera to get a drink of water.

(Right) Karolyn looks quite content in the arms of the Producer-Director, Leslie Fenton

8

Publicity Photo showing Karolyn with a matching Shirley Temple doll.

(Top) The cast of **Pardon My Past**. (From left) William Demerest, Harry Davenport, Fred MacMurray, Marguerite Chapman, Rita Johnson, MacMurray, and Akim Tamiroff. Standing in front, looking quite coy, is little Karolyn.

(Lower left) As Harry Davenport, who plays Karolyn's Grandfather, sleeps, she has to try looking through his glasses in this publicity photo.

(Lower right) Fred MacMurray helps his screen daughter, Karolyn, load blocks in a wagon for the movie.

Karolyn
Grimes looks
on as
Rita Johnson
and Fred
MacMurray
have a
serious
conversation

Blue Skies

Produced By: Paramount n
Director: Stuart Heisler
Release date: July 25, 1946
104 minutes, color

Stars: Bing Crosby, Fred Astaire, Joan Caufield, Billy De Wolfe

Karolyn's role: [Filmed September 6-8, 1945] Eighth in the credits, she plays Mary Elizabeth, the daughter of the Crosby Character

Comment: Twenty Irving Berlin tunes add up to pleasant entertainment about a dancer and nightclub owner wooing the same girl. *Blue Skies* is a lot of fun to watch. The songs are engaging; Astaire's dance segments are superbly choreographed. Karolyn's segment with Crosby singing "Getting Nowhere" is a genuine high spot. The only real problem is a dated, interminably long would-be comedy routine by De Wolfe.

Karolyn's Comments: "They were getting so desperate in their search for a little girl to play the part of Bing Crosby's daughter, Mary Elizabeth, that they were considering putting a blonde wig on one of his sons. Then I came along, and I got the part.

Bing Crosby liked to play practical jokes and sometimes they included me. Jerry Colonna used to stop by the set and they would laugh and joke around. At the end of the filming, Bing sent me (as a gift) the outfit that I wore in the movie.

A couple of years later, I was on the lot at Paramount Studios when I saw Bing across the street. He called to me. I went over to chat with him. I told him that I had a brand new dog and that I had named him Bing because he howled all night. Bing got a good laugh out of that."

Trivia: Look for a stage hand played by Frank Faylen who, one year later, became Ernie the cab driver in *It's A Wonderful Life* and went on to play Dobie's father in the TV sitcom *The Many Loves of Dobie Gillis.*

Photo left: Fred Astaire, "Putting On The Ritz" in a remarkable dance segment from the movie "Blue Skies."

Being in the arms of movie legends was nothing new to Karolyn as Bing Crosby holds his movie daughter in his arms.

Karolyn (Mary-Elizabeth) persuades Bing Crosby (who plays her father), to sing her a song before she goes to bed.

(Above)
Karolyn and
Bing Crosby
share a secret on
the set of the
making of
Blue Skies.

(Right)
Karolyn gets
acquainted with
the composer
Irving Berlin
on the
Blue Skies set.

Director, Stuart Heisler, coaches Bing Crosby and Karolyn as they rehearse the song "Getting Nowhere." The song was composed by Irving Berlin with Karolyn in mind.

16

Karolyn reunites with her film father, Bing Crosby, who she hasn't seen in four years.

5 year old
Karolyn
poses
on the set of
Blue Skies.

Sister Kenny

Produced By: RKO Radio Pictures
Director: Dudley Nicols
Release date: September 28, 1946
118 minutes, black and white

Stars: Rosalind Russell, Alexander Know, Dean Jagger, Philip Merivale

Karolyn's role: [Filmed between November] 1945 and January 1946) She plays a polio victim named Carolyn.

Comment: Story of the famous Australian nurse and her fight against infantile paralysis. Frequently stirring drama. The sincerity and skill of the Australian nurse played by Russell are credible, but to its credit, the movie stops short of fully endorsing her unconventional approach to treating childhood polio. The ambiguity of the story nicely prompts a desire to read the autobiography upon which the film was based. Excellently acted.

Karolyn's Comments: "When I was a little girl, every one was rightfully afraid of the dreadful disease, polio. My mother always cautioned me about regarding germs. I was especially conscious of the disabling effects of polio. So, when I played a little girl who had contracted the disease, as if I could imagine how it was for a lot of children who were not so lucky as I."

Trivia: Another *It's A Wonderful Life* actress, Beulah Bondi (George Bailey's mother), appears in *Sister Kenny* in a brief supporting role.

Left: Rosalind Russell as Sister Kenny

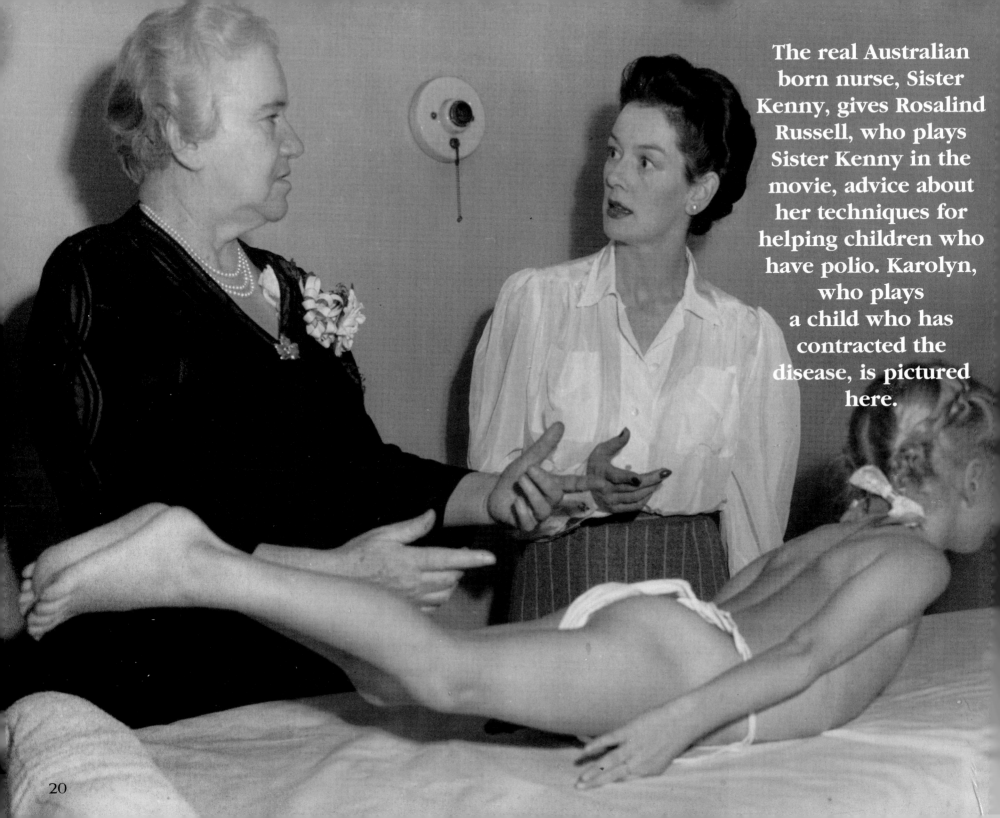

The real Australian born nurse, Sister Kenny, gives Rosalind Russell, who plays Sister Kenny in the movie, advice about her techniques for helping children who have polio. Karolyn, who plays a child who has contracted the disease, is pictured here.

Rosalind Russell portrays Sister Kenny in one of her many travels from the film *Sister Kenny*.

It's a Wonderful Life

Produced By: Liberty Film/RKO Radio Pictures
Director: Frank Capra
Release date: December 19, 1946
129 minutes, black and white

Stars: James Stewart, Donna Reed, Lionel Barrymore, Thomas Mitchell, Henry Travers, Beulah Bondi, Gloria Grahame

Karolyn's role: [Filmed in 1946] She is 33rd in the credits. She plays Zuzu Bailey.

Comment: One of the best movies—if not the best—of all time, untouchable in its grasp of the desires and principles that fuel the American spirit. George Bailey, who constantly confronts the roadblocks of life in the small town of Bedford Falls, finds himself at the end of his rope. Clarence (Travers), the angel, makes it possible to show George what life in this town would be like without him. Stewart gives one of his finest performances as George Bailey. The film was Frank Capra's favorite among his own films. This is a film guaranteed to prompt tears of joy. Considering the movies power, its 30-year dormancy is remarkable, and its revival an enduring gift.

Karolyn's Comments: "On the set of *It's a Wonderful Life*, in Culver City, I had the chance to see and feel the wonder of snow for the first time. Being from the land of sunshine, it was a tremendous fascination which gave me a whole different feeling about Christmas and families.

While working in the Christmas atmosphere that permeated the week that I was there, I played and interacted with the other children. My day wasn't complete without chasing Jimmy Hawkins, little Tommy, around the movie set. Perhaps this was the first time it occurred to me that Christmas with a brother and sister was something that I really had not experienced. Today, the Bailey kids as adults, have a special bond because of the film. I feel as if I really do have brothers and a sister.

When I flubbed a line one time, I remember Jimmy Stewart said to me, 'it's all right to make mistakes and don't you feel bad. You'll get it right the next take,' and I did."

Trivia: Though they never shared screen time in this film, Karolyn and Bobby Anderson (the young George Bailey) acted together in a key segment from another Christmas/angel film released one year later, *The Bishop's Wife*.

Photo left: Standing outside the Bailey house, with his dreams once again dashed, George (Jimmy Stewart) looks at his travel brochures.

(Above)
After Mr. Potter (Lionel Barrymore) has spun a devious plot, George (Jimmy Stewart) tells him he is "nothing but a scurvy little spider."

(Right)
George offers Mary (Donna Reed) her belt from her robe. Both are hanging on to their clothes.

From left: Thomas Mitchell (Uncle Billy, Carol Coombs (Janie), Donna Reed (Mary), Jimmy Stewart (George), Karolyn Grimes (Zuzu), Larry Simms (Peter), Sarah Edwards (Mrs. Hatch), Beaulah Bondi (Mrs. Bailey) and next to Janie stands little Tommy (Jimmy Hawkins).

(Above)
Jimmy Stewart as George wishes to win a million dollars as he stands next ot Mr. Gower, played by H.B. Warner.
(Right)
Back in his real life, George finds Zuzu's Petals in his pocket and shows them to a confused Bert (Ward Bond).

The cover of "Newsweek" Magazine, December 30, 1946 shows the final scene from the movie, *It's a Wonderful Life*.

(Above)
Mary (Donna Reed) shows George her rendition of the memory of the night he told her he would "lasso the moon" and give it to her.
(Right)
Mary looks on as George embraces Zuzu and family in this publicity photo from the film.

A cast photo showing the winter scene of the town of Bedford Falls.

Mary and George look fondly at their precious little Zuzu who has just uttered the line, "Look, daddy, teacher says, 'every time a bell rings an angel gets his wings.'"

(Above)
Frank Capra and Jimmy Stewart are all smiles in this publicity photo for the film *It's a Wonderful Life.*
(Left)
Cutting up between takes, Jimmy Stewart laughs with the cast. The photo is autographed by Jimmy Stewart "To Zuzu–with my love."

To Zuzu
With my love.
Jimmy Stewart

Karolyn played
Zuzu whose
name was derived
from the product
called "Zu Zu
Ginger Snaps" by
the National
Biscuit Company.

The Private Affairs of Bel Ami

Produced By: United Artists
Director: Albert Lewin
Release date: February 25, 1947
112 minutes, black and white

Stars: George Sanders, Angela Lansbury, Ann Dvorak, John Carradine

Karolyn's role: [Filmed in the fall of 1946] She is 17th in the credits and plays Laurine.

Comment: Sanders plays a thoroughly believable scoundrel and cad. He uses and discards people to propel his selfish desires. Acting by Sanders and Lansbury commands interest, as does the Parisian setting. Karolyn does her best to warm the heart of Sanders, but it's questionable whether his character even has one.

Karolyn's Comments: "Beautiful Angela Lansbury was only nineteen years old when I played her daughter in this film. I remember spending hours having my hair fixed for this one. All those ringlets took a lot of time to get just right. It seemed like I was sitting in that chair getting hair done for hours. I really liked the dresses I got to wear, they were so fancy. The set for the house that I lived in for this film was just so dreamy and feminine. I loved all the drapes and the frilly decor. I carried around a wooden soldier during the playtime. The room sets were elegant and I had to play the piano. I enjoyed that very much. I wasn't allowed to hang around with George Sanders. It seems he didn't care much for children."

Trivia: Angela Lansbury was only nineteen years old when she played Karolyn's mother in this film

Comments: The precursors to Sanders' *tour de force* as Addison Dewitt in the 1950's film *All About Eve* are on full display here.

Top left: A lobby card showing a tender scene between Angela Lansbury and George Sanders from the movie.

Lower left: A poster advertising the movie

Karolyn, wearing a robe during her free time so that she didn't soil her costumes, plays with some toys her mother provided.

(Above)
Karolyn as she
played the
character, Laurine,
in the movie
*The Private
Affairs
of Bel Ami.*
(Left)
Angela Lansbury
as Karolyn's
mother exchanges
glances with
George Sanders.

(Above)
Karolyn performs in this publicity photo from the film *The Private Affairs of Bel Ami.*

(Right)
Practicing the technique of crossing over on the piano, Karolyn shows her ability with the ivories.

35

In a behind the scenes photo, Angela Lansbury works with Karolyn's hair.

36

A rare picture of Karolyn and her mother Martha checking out one of the garments in wardrobe that Karolyn will wear in the film.

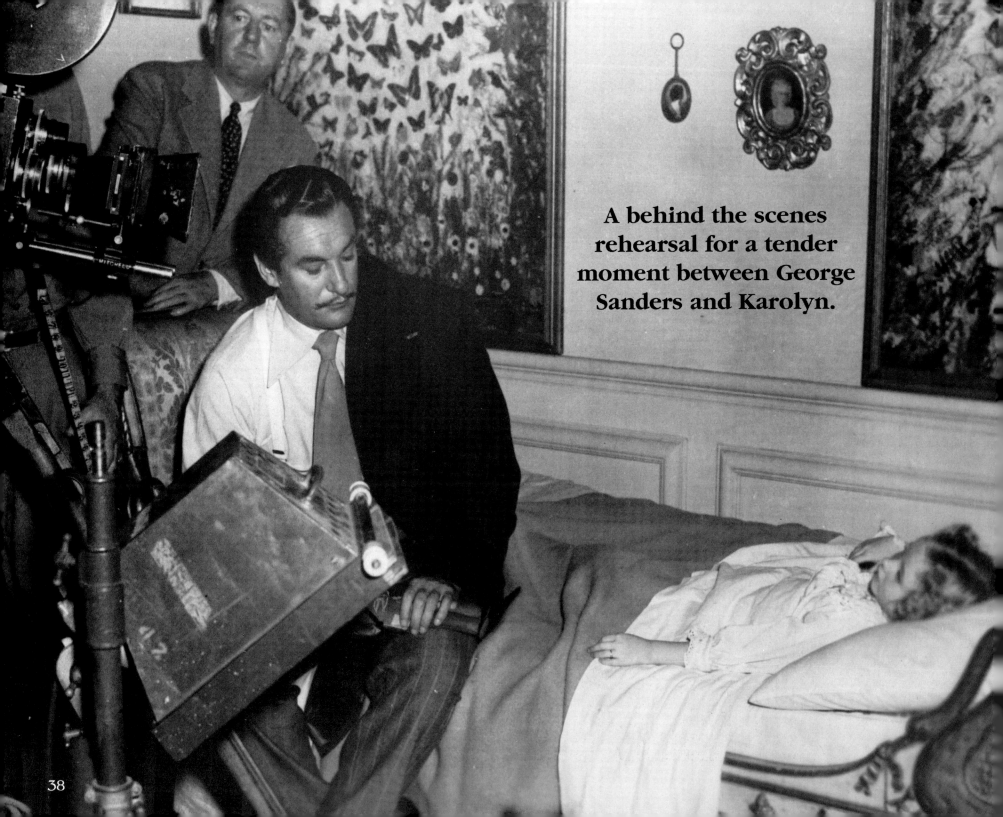

A behind the scenes rehearsal for a tender moment between George Sanders and Karolyn.

Sweet and Low

Produced By: Paramount
Director: Jerry Hopper
Release date: March 28th 1947
19 minutes (short subject) color

Stars: Richard Webb, Catherine Craig, Willie Mastin Trio Featuring Sammy Davis, Jr.

Karolyn's role: [Filmed July 31-August 3, 1946] She is third in the credits, plays Tammie, as detailed in in an early script under the working title *Masque Ball*.

Comment: This short subject may be a gem. As the film is apparently unavailable for viewing, it's hard to say. The innocence and honesty of Karolyn's character help her parents achieve what they, with their adult sensibilities, cannot achieve by themselves. It's a well-worn theme, but always worth revisiting if played out well.

Karolyn's Comments: "I was always in bed in the films I was in. For this film, I really got to act as if I was sleepy. Can you imagine what it was like for a little child to lie still for a long time while they took so many different scenes one after the other? I got pretty good at acting as if I were asleep."

Trivia: *Sweet and Low* could be the earliest appearance on film of the legendary Davis, who was 20 at the time. (His earliest feature film, *The Benny Goodman Story*, came nine years later, in 1955.) This could be a better reason to make *Sweet and Low* available to the public?

Right: Karolyn shares a sleepy moment with Griff Barnett in "Sweet and Low."

Griff Barnett, as Marlan Kane the composer, reads a story to Karolyn in *Sweet and Low.*

40

Karolyn gets tucked in for the night by her mother (Catherine Craig) in the film *Sweet and Low.*

WITH LOVE TO KAROLYN —

Catherine Craig

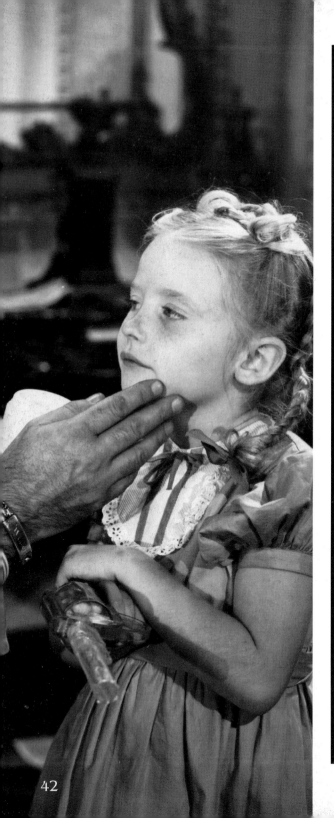

Philo Vance's Gamble

Produced By: Producers Releasing Corporation
Director: Basil Wrangell
Release date: April 1947
62 minutes, black and white

Stars: Alan Curtis, Terry Austin, Frank Jenks, Tala Birell

Karolyn's role: [Filmed sometime in December 1946 and January 1947] She plays Pam Roberts.

Comment: Vance tackles the Mob and investigates three murders. Weapons emerge ominously from behind curtains, secrets galore, all on a dark, murderous night—this is the B-movie detective formula played to a T. What brightens and shakes up the proceedings, though, is the important plot presence of a little girl who likes to surprise strangers by brandishing a toy gun. Made of plastic, the gun is really a shell to hold rock candy, and, in this case, a stolen emerald. This one is fun all around.

Karolyn's Comments: "Alan Curtis was a very handsome man who played the famous detective, Philo Vance, in several movies. I got to work with him in *Philo Vance's Gamble*. I was playing stick-up with that little plastic gun, I got pretty good at 'Hands up mister' actions. One time I hid behind a tree and jumped out with my little weapon. I scared Alan Curtis. At least he acted as if he really was scared. So when it came time in the next scene for him to rub this awful smelling cream on my face, he just kept rubbing it on my cheeks. He said, 'I bet you won't want to scare me again.' We all had a good laugh."

Trivia: Less-known than other fictional private eyes, the Philo Vance character nevertheless headlined 14 films from 1929 to 1947.

Left: Alan Curtis (as Philo Vance) rubs cream on Karolyn's face. From the film, "Philo Vance's Gamble."

Karolyn watches
as Alan Curtis (Philo Vance)
takes a piece of candy
out of her plastic gun as his
assistant looks on.

43

Karolyn brandishes a gun at Frank Jenks, a police detective. Alan Curtis as Philo Vance smiles because he knows the gun is plastic.

Alan Curtis stands ready to wipe the dirt off of Karolyn's face as she tries to scare Frank Jenks.

Posters advertising the movie's release

Mother Wore Tights

Produced By: 20th Century Fox
Director: Walter Lang
Release date: August 19, 1947
107 minutes, color

Stars: Betty Grable, Dan Dailey, Mona Freeman

Karolyn's role: (Filmed sometime from October 1946 through January 1947) She plays young Iris (Betty Grable's daughter.)

Comment: Even though producers of this musical let too much plot get in the way of the songs, this movie is still colorful, energetic and fun. The favorite pinup girl of the '40s, Betty Grable's name on the marquee was insurance that any film in which she appeared would be a box-office hit. Most noted for her sensational legs, Grable's picture was plastered in the lockers of our boys in the service. They carried these pictures with them to the front. The girls back home didn't mind. Betty, though gorgeous, was so very likable. She won the hearts of the women as well. *Mother Wore Tights*, one of Betty Grable's most popular films, was Betty's personal favorite.

It is packed with nostalgic moments and memorable song-and-dance numbers. Celebrating the life and times of the vaudeville circuit, this affectionate, nostalgic tale traces the love affair of a beautiful dancer (Grable) and a comedian (Dan Dailey), who marry and raise a family while continuing to perform on the road. Filled with sketches, charming vignettes and sensational musical interludes, *Mother Wore Tights* is the first of four films pairing Grable with her favorite co-star, Dan Dailey. Alfred Newman's Oscar-winning musical score provides the perfect tone for this Technicolor treat. Rounding out the cast are Ruth Nelson and young Mona Freeman. Family entertainment at its best!

Karolyn's Comments: "I must have a very common face because I was cast as the daughter of many movie legends. I actually was privileged to have a view up close of those famous legs of Betty Grable. In this movie I am in old-fashioned underwear, and, for the first time, I knew what it was like to wear pantaloons! It was a very small part but I enjoyed it because I got to be bossy to my little sister in the movie."

Trivia: Remember Senior Wences' charming ventriloquism act, a mainstay of TV's *Ed Sullivan Show*? An early version appears here.

Betty Grable and Dan Dailey as they appeared in their vaudeville act from the movie, *Mother Wore Tights.*

Unconquered

Produced By: Paramount
Director: Cecil B. DeMille
Release date: October 3, 1947
146 minutes, color

Stars: Gary Cooper, Paulette Goddard, Howard Da Silva, Boris Karloff, Cecil Kellaway

Karolyn's role: [Filmed in the fall of 1946] She is 133rd in the cast list, plays a "little girl" lying dead in her mothers arms.

Comment: Fans of Gary Cooper and Goddard (once Charles Chaplan's paramour and co-star) will enjoy these stars trying to bring some credibility to this depiction of pre-Revolutionary War America. White man vs Indian in 1763, this film has tons of action. Plenty of movement and colorful acting are the total assets of this mammoth production. Ultimately, it's as lifeless as the tiny role played by Karolyn. DeMille never did learn that less is more.

Karolyn's Comments: "By this time I was used to playing asleep so playing dead wasn't so bad. There were so many people on the set for this film that, at times I thought I would be squashed. It was the largest cast I ever worked with."

Trivia: Bert and Ernie, from *It's a Wonderful Life*, each show up in one of Karolyn's films. This time it's Ward Bond (Bert the cop), who has a meaty supporting role in this colonial tale.

Left: Gary Cooper with Boris Karloff (as Indian) in a scene from the movie.

Killed in battle,
Karolyn lies
lifeless in the
arms of
her mother.

A photo of a portion of the massive cast Cecil B. DeMille used for this film epic *Unconquered.*

50

The Bishop's Wife
Produced By: Samuel Goldwyn Productions/RKO Pictures
Director: Henry Koster
Release date: December 25, 1947
108 minutes, black and white

Stars: Cary Grant, Loretta Young, David Niven, Monty Wooley, James Gleason

Karolyn's role: [Filmed in the summer of 1947] She is ninth in the credits, playing Debby Brougham.

Comment: Grant, as an angel, comes to earth in answer to a prayer from a bishop played by David Niven. His presence profoundly affects many people, especially Niven who gets a lesson in priorities. *The Bishop's Wife* ranks with *It's a Wonderful Life* as a classic. The actors' chemistry enhances this angel fable, and the outcome is never quite certain until the end. Delightful sequences fill the film, from the hilarious symbolism of Niven stuck to a donor's chair, to a warming harp interlude and a stunning hymn from the Mitchell Boys Choir. Karolyn is in the thick of it all.

Karolyn's Comments: "As in *It's a Wonderful Life*, the winter scenes for this film were filmed in June, forcing the creation of the artificial snow settings. A soundstage with 10 miles of pipes that were flooded and frozen served as a glazed-over lake for the ice skating segments. Cary Grant was extremely bright and he didn't have to work on his lines that much, and I think he was bored. He could ice skate quite well and pulled me around on a sled while he skated during our lunchtime. He would come and get me and say, "Let's go for a little spin Karolyn." I never thought of him as a handsome movie idol because I was too young to realize that. I saw these people all the time, and I didn't really think too much about it. They were just like everybody else. They were just my friends. The movie's snow resulted from the shaving of 20 tons of ice into tiny flakes, allowing for the creation of realistic snowballs, snowmen and slush.

I had to wear a wool snowsuit, and it rubbed against my face. Since I'm allergic to wool, I found that was quite uncomfortable.

The Bishop's Wife premiered on November 25, 1947 in London, England at the Odeon Theatre, as a Royal Command Film Performance for Their Majesties, the King and Queen, to benefit the Cinematography Trade Benevolent Fund. In Los Angeles, *The Bishop's Wife* opened on Christmas night as a charity premiere at Hollywood's Carthy Circle Theater. I remember being interviewed on the radio that night. I though that was pretty special. The next morning I heard my mother comment that I had gotten a good critic from the *Hollywood Citizen News* for my 'vivid characterization.'

RKO used me to advertise the film in the press book including a photo of Cary Grant holding me on his lap and reading a story from a new children's book. The story was called "You and The United Nations." Theaters were urged to build window displays around the book, described as 'unique in style, containing human interest copy and profusely illustrated.' The studio's alignment of the movie with such a political concern as the United Nations was unusual but it likely reflected the national hopes for world peace following the UN's post-World War II formation and cleverly reinforced the movie's underlying theme of community harmony.

But the best of all was the angel doll! They fashioned an angel doll like the one Loretta Young found on my bed, supposedly left by Dudley the angel. The doll was called "Wee Bit of Heaven." They would dress me up and I would go in limousines to department stores to autograph these dolls. I would sign dolls for about two hours at each appearance. That was really work but fun to do because I got to meet so many people."

Trivia: For the magical skating sequence, professional skaters were used, their faces covered with masks in the images of Grant and Young

THE HOLLYWOOD DOLL COMPANY presents
THE LUCKY STAR DOLL
inspired by the SAMUEL GOLDWYN production starring
Cary **GRANT** · Loretta **YOUNG** · David **NIVEN**
"The Bishop's Wife"

Karolyn Grimes

This photo showing a sleeping Karolyn was included in every angel doll box advertising *The Bishop's Wife.* Karolyn's autograph appears in the left corner where she signed it at the age of 7.

Next page: Gary Grant convinces Loretta Young that a crying Karoyn will be just fine. In the lower left corner, Loretta Young comments to Karolyn, "It was fun wasn't it."

To Karolyn
It was fun
wasn't it?
Loretta Young

53

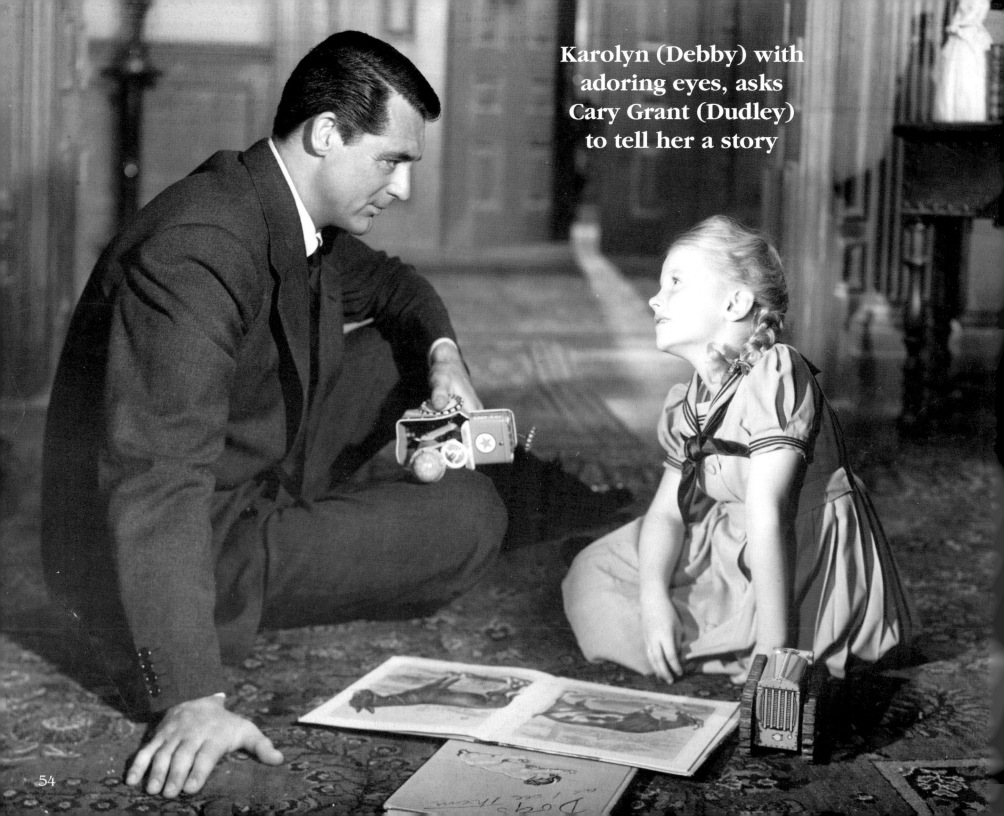

Karolyn (Debby) with
adoring eyes, asks
Cary Grant (Dudley)
to tell her a story

54

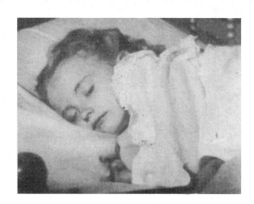

Karolyn tells her mother, Loretta Young, and Cary Grant she is having a wonderful time playing in the snow. All smiles, Elsa Lancaster looks on.

Right: Cary Grant, David Niven and Loretta Young in a comical taxi ride.

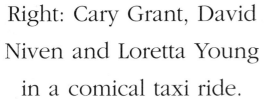

Left: This scene was never used in the movie, but protrays Karolyn's genuine affection for Grant

Cary Grant reads to some of the children in this publicity photo. Karolyn is the muffet sitting on his lap.

Cary Grant defending little Karolyn against Bobbie Anderson (third from the right), who played the young George Bailey in the movie, *It's a Wonderful Life*. The setting is an example of the winter wonderland that was created for the movie.

Above: Karolyn looking on as Grant and Young converse in the foyer.

Right: Behind the scene direction given to Karolyn by Henry Koster (the Director) lying on the floor with Grant looking on.

Left: Cary Grant sharing the story of David and Goliath with Karolyn as David Niven, Loretta Young and the Bishop's secretary look on.

Opposite page: One of the lobby cards advertising the movie. Note the wording bills the movie as *Cary and the Bishop's Wife*. The final release title was *The Bishop's Wife*.

One of those really rare pictures that leave you with a wonderful glow!

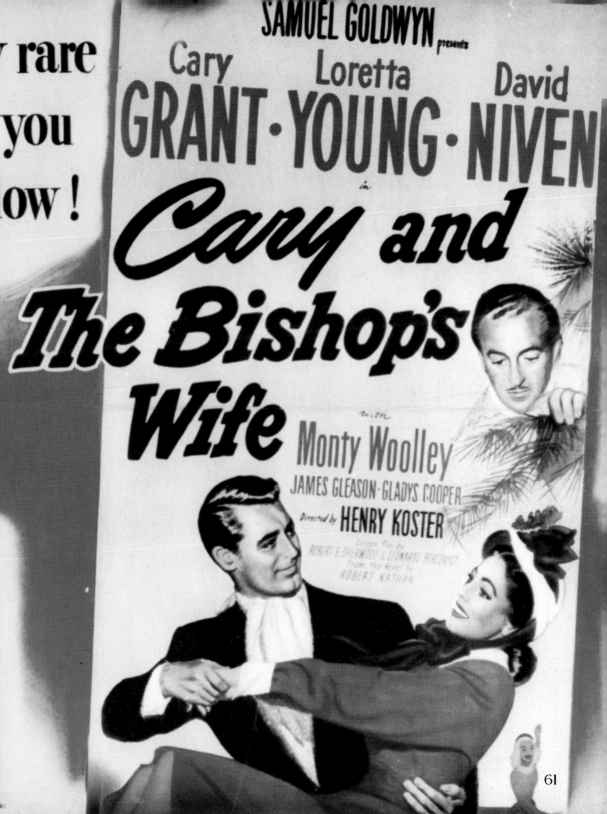

SAMUEL GOLDWYN presents

Cary **GRANT** · Loretta **YOUNG** · David **NIVEN**

in

Cary and The Bishop's Wife

with Monty Woolley

JAMES GLEASON · GLADYS COOPER

Directed by HENRY KOSTER

Screen Play by ROBERT E. SHERWOOD & LEONARDO BERCOVICI
From the Novel by ROBERT NATHAN

61

Below: Karolyn signed autographs at Bullock's Home Store, in Los Angeles, to promote sales of the "Wee Bit of Heaven Doll."

Come to Our Autograph Party!
IN PERSON . . .

Karolyn Grimes

Child star of Samuel Goldwyn's production "The Bishop's Wife" will be at Bullock's Tuesday, December 30th, from 1 to 3 p.m.

Doll Section, Fifth Floor, Bullock's Broadway Building

See this "Wee Bit of Heaven" doll, inspired by the angel in "The Bishop's Wife," on sale in our Doll Section, 1.95

TRinity 1911, Store Hours 9:30 to 5:30

Bullock's
DOWNTOWN

Above: Monty Wooley (the Professor) exchanging gifts with Loretta Young. Note the angel on top of the tree, very much like the doll that Karolyn had on her bed.

Albuquerque

Produced By: Paramount - Clarion
Director: Ray Enright
Release date: February 20, 1948
89 minutes, color

Stars: Randolph Scott, Barbara Britton, Gabby Hayes, Lon Chaney Jr., Catherine Craig

Karolyn's role: [Filmed sometime from March through June of 1947] She is 10th in the credits and plays Myrtle Walton.

Comment: As western as they come, *Albuquerque* packs clichés by the stagecoach load. A typical western centered around the nephew who revolts against his uncle's ways, it's much more fun that most of its kind, thanks in large part to Karolyn, whose segments never fail to liven up matters. The best instance comes as she earnestly tries, through prison bars, to convince Scott to break out of jail. Beautifully filmed in color.

Karolyn's Comments: "This was my first western picture. It was filmed on location at the Circle J Ranch in the San Fernando Valley north of Los Angeles. For our lunches, they had a huge table loaded with catered foods. There were all kinds of different delicious dishes. It was fun to taste a little of this and a little of that. But I couldn't help noticing that Gabby Hayes had the same meal every day for lunch. I thought it was awful, so I never forgot. He had a glass filled with buttermilk and cornbread. That is all he ate.

I got to ride in stagecoaches and on horses. I even had my own pet burro.

One of the things that stands out in my memory of making this film was a fierce fight between Randolph Scott and Lon Chaney Jr. Through the eyes of a little girl, Lon Chaney Jr. was a very scary guy. He was tall and rough looking and sounding. He really gave me the creeps because I kept seeing the Wolfman. That was the character that he had made famous. He told me I was ugly because I had freckles. I always thought he was right.

During the fight scene, he had to make fake blood run out of his mouth and nose. He showed me the capsule that he put in his mouth and then squeezed at the right moment. He hid the movement of his hand by falling down."

Trivia: Catherine Craig, after this movie, relinquished her 10 year career for marriage to Robert Preston. She was also in another film with Karolyn, *Sweet and Low*.

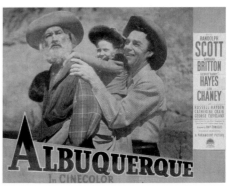

Karolyn
cradles the
movie's
mascot,
a beautiful
butterfly.

(Above)
Karolyn, as
Myrtle,
pleads with the
judge to pardon
her friend
Randolph Scott
(Cole).

(Right)
Karolyn (Myrtle),
is preparing to
say good-bye to
her friend
Randolph, (Cole).

(Top Right)
Gabby Hayes
(Juke), tells
Karolyn,
"You'd better
skidattle home...
run along now."

(Bottom Right)
Scott entertains
Karolyn by
turning his left
hand into
a puppet during
a long stage
coach ride.

(Opposite Page)
Karolyn looking
radiant after
being rescued
in a runaway
stage by
Randolph Scott.

A TRUE STORY OF SECRET TREASURE!

COLUMBIA PICTURES presents

GLENN FORD · IDA LUPINO

LUST FOR GOLD

with GIG YOUNG · William PRINCE · Edgar BUCHANAN

Screen Play by Ted Sherdeman and Richard English

Produced and Directed by S. SYLVAN SIMON

Lust for Gold

Produced By: Columbia
Director: Sylvan Simon
Release date: May 31, 1949
90 minutes, black and white

Stars: Ida Lupino, Glenn Ford, Gig Young, Paul Ford

Karolyn's role: [Filmed in late 1949] She plays young Martha Bannister.

Comment: Excellent film showing how greed and evil take over and ruin basically good people with edge-of-seat suspense and fine performances by all. The narration in this self-titled "documentary western" strains to emphasize the film's real-life story; at times the legendary hype seems a bit melodramatic. But, as Saturday matinee fare for impressionable kids, this fills the bill. In the tussle between greed and the secrets of Superstition Mountain, the outcome is never in question. Ford, Lupino and half a dozen bit players, plus the film's flashback structure, make *Lust for Gold* interesting nonetheless.

Karolyn's Comments: "I fretted for three days because the studio told me that they were going to blow onion dust in my eyes to make me cry. I was afraid it would really hurt. When the time came for the shoot, they blew the onion dust in my eyes, I cried, and it did not hurt a bit. Then, as it turned out, that entire segment was cut from the film."

Trivia: Paul Ford plays a present-day sheriff, and portraying one of his deputies is Jay Silverheels, the man who played Tonto for many years on TV's *The Lone Ranger*.

Above Left: Poster advertising the film.

Left: Ida Lupino and Glenn Ford in a Publicity photo for the film, "Lust for Gold."

Karolyn and Glenn Ford in a scene from the film, *Lust for Gold.*

69

If **YOU** are interested
in picking up
$ 20,000,000 IN GOLD
see Lust For Gold!

The clues are in the picture... a violent but true story of jealousy, murder and buried treasure.

LUST FOR GOLD actually happened!
It's based on the historical records
of the State of Arizona.

COLUMBIA PICTURES presents

GLENN FORD · IDA LUPINO
LUST FOR GOLD

with GIG YOUNG · William Prince · Edgar Buchanan
Screen Play by Ted Sherdeman and Richard English
Produced and Directed by S. SYLVAN SIMON

Lobby Card advertising the movie, *Lust for Gold.*

A troubled
Glenn Ford
prepares to
protect
his claim.

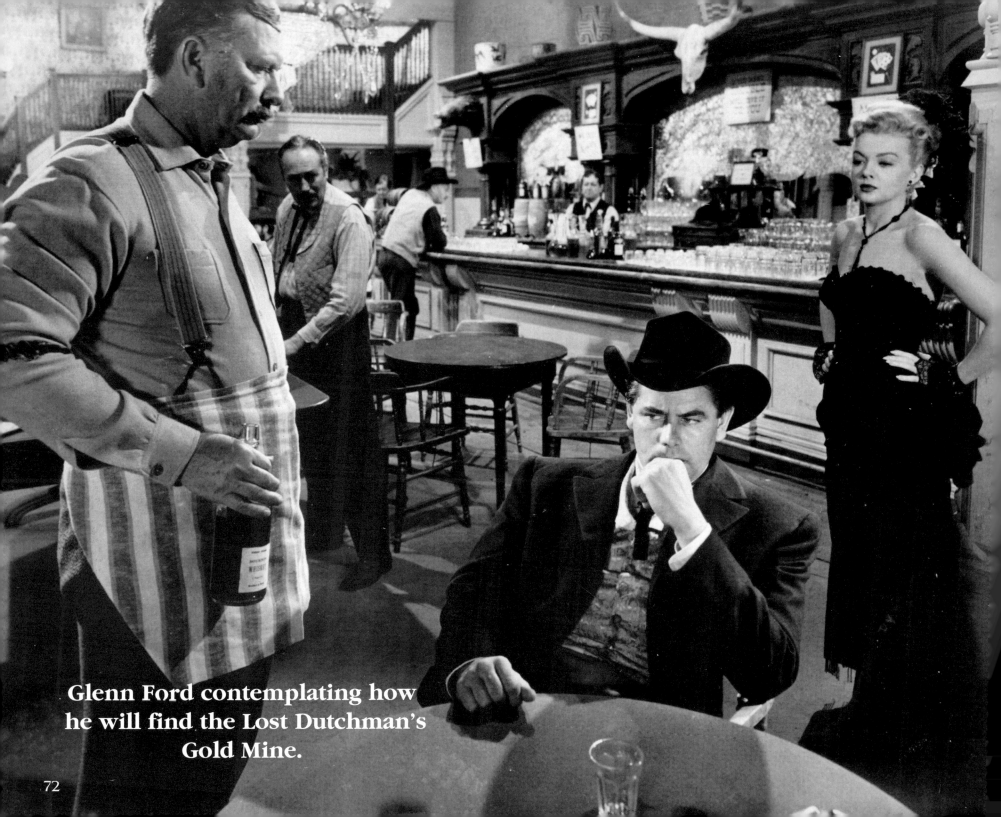

Glenn Ford contemplating how he will find the Lost Dutchman's Gold Mine.

Rio Grande

Produced By: Republic Studios
Director: John Ford
Release date: November 2, 1950
105 minutes, black and white

Stars: John Wayne, Maureen O'Hara, Ben Johnson, Harry Carey Jr., Victor McLaglen, Claude Jarman Jr.

Karolyn's role: [Filmed in Jun and July 1950] She 13th in the credits, and plays Margaret Mary.

Comment: Tough cavalry commander (Wayne) awaits orders to cross a river so that he can clean up marauding Indians. John Ford's epic western has beautiful scenery, good action, and plenty of drama as the commander also comes to grips with his feelings for his son, who is one of his newest enlistees. Wayne and O'Hara are an intriguing match, and the intertwining activity of young, inexperienced cavalrymen and their older, crusty counterparts is far more complex than in typical good-guy / bad-guy tales. The *Sons of the Pioneers* add symbolism and gallantry to the proceedings.

Karolyn's Comments: "For Three week we filmed part of the movie in a small town in Utah called Moab. I got to fly in an airplane for the first time. My mother had always taught me that movie stars were just regular people. Yet, here was this very tall and gruff man, named John Wayne, whose booming voice made me want to laugh and to hide all at the same time. His presence was immense. He captivated everyone with his sense of humor and sparkling eyes. He called me "Little Miss Karolyn."

The location was at a ranch on the Colorado River. There was quicksand in the river and there were all kinds of snakes. It was desolate and yet beautiful. It was like living in a time in the past. Once when it was my turn to work, I rode in a covered wagon being chased by Indians. A truck with a camera was filming alongside as the Indians and horses flew by. It was all very exciting. Of course, I was captured and held captive!

While we were there, the Korean conflict broke out. It became difficult to have supplies shipped in because the government was commandeering many airplanes. I turned ten years old while we were there and my birthday happens to be the 4th of July. John Wayne managed to have $300 worth of fireworks flown in and he had a huge birthday cake baked for me. The cake and all the fireworks were taken to the bluffs of the Colorado River where the cast and crew had one great party. It was a Happy Birthday to Karolyn. I will always remember Wayne's generosity and big heart."

Trivia: The best horseman of film's young bucks is Ben Johnson, better known to latter-day audiences for his weathered, Academy Award-winning supporting role in 1971's *The Last Picture Show.*

Right: Maureen O'Hara plays Kathleen and John Wayne plays her husband Col. Kirby Yorke in this publicity photo.

To Karolyn, My Little Sweetheart, With Love, Claude

Above: Claude Jarman, Jr. plays
John Wayne's son, Private Yorke, in the film.

Below: Karolyn as Margaret Mary
in the film, *Rio Grande*.

A group picture of the *Sons of the Pioneers*, who performed throughout the film. Upper left, is Shug Fischer who played the stuttering bugler in the film. Far right, is Ken Curtis the lead singer who played Festus in the TV drama *Gunsmoke.* His father-in-law was John Ford, the director of *Rio Grande.*

An action scene depicting Indians getting ready to attack the wagon carrying the children from the fort.

Ben Johnson used no stunt men to show his skill at Roman Riding in this scene from *Rio Grande*.

Col. Yorke (John Wayne)
leads the charge in an effort to save the
captive children in the mission that has been
captured by the Indians.

John Wayne, as Col. Yorke, surveys his prospects of crossing the Rio Grande River, whch in reality is the Colorado River.

Victor Mclaglen gives instructions to the trio from left, Ben Johnson, Harry Carey, Jr. and Claude Jarman, Jr.

From left: Chill Wills, as the crusty doctor, salutes the soldiers with J. Carrol Naish, John Wayne and Maureen O'Hara. Karolyn stands, with parasol in hand, watching the proceedings

Honeychile

Produced By: Republic Pictures
Director: R.G Springsteen
Release date: November 12, 1951
90 minutes, color

Stars: Judy Canova, Eddie Foy, Jr., Alan Hale, Jr., Walter Catlett

Karolyn's role: [Filmed in November 1950] She is sixth in the credits and plays the part of Effie.

Comment: Laced with cleverly written gags, this, by mistake, is pure corn all the way. There's a big crisis as a music publishing company has pressed 200,000 records of a love song attributed to a famous composer. Alas, it was the song that the country-livin' Canova had written and submitted to the company. Karolyn has more screen time in this than in any other film. She exhibits a naturalness as the niece who takes care of Canova's household. The film is a showcase for Canova's comedy and musical ability.

Karolyn's Comments: "Judy Canova played my aunt in this film. I played a farm girl quite well because I had a natural little twang in my speech. I always felt like I was a little too old for this part. My body was changing rapidly and I was not supposed to be full figured. So my mother designed and sewed a binder for me to wear while we filmed.

Judy had a great voice and she just plain enjoyed singing. She could do anything with her face. Her expressions were so funny."

Trivia: The man in Canova's life is none other than Alan Hale, Jr., who played the Skipper in TV's *Gilligan's Island*.

Left: Judy Canova singing the song, "Tutti Frutti." A happy Karolyn participates in the number.

A lobby card showing the comedian Judy Canova advertising her new movie, *Honeychile*.

Alan Hale, Jr. gets a surprise and laughs as a box of frogs spit in his face. Judy Canova and Eddy Foy, Jr. enjoy the moment.

Judy Canova belts one of her famous songs in this grand finale of *Honeychile*. Karolyn, with Judy on the bandstand, is peeking out from under the white cowboy hat on the far right.

Left: Karolyn and her movie brother prepare to set up the scene for Judy Canova to sing the song, "Tutti Frutti" to the Ice Cream Man, played by Fuzzy Knight.

Right: Eddy Foy, Jr. pulls the arm of Judy Canova, maneuvering to get her attention in a scene from the movie, *Honeychile.*

Hans Christian Anderson

Produced By: RKO Radio Pictures
Director: Charles Vidor
Release date: November 25, 1952
120 minutes, color

Stars: Danny Kaye, Farley Granger, Jeanmaire

Karolyn's role: [Filmed in May 1952] She plays a match girl.

Comment: Kaye, the teller of fairy tales, falls in love with a beautiful ballerina. The ebullient Danny Kaye is a delight as Hans, particularly in his singing scenes with youngsters. The music and colorful sets are ideal children's entertainment with some spectacular fantasy scenes.

Karolyn's Comments: "This bit part was a blink of the eyelids. But I did get to be with Danny Kaye for a couple of days, AND I got to sing. Danny loved to sing, and he was always walking around singing his lilnes. I asked him if that was the way he learned to memorize the words, and he said, "Yes, it was."

Trivia: Karolyn's last film role is also her shortest. Unlike most of her other films in which she played the only child, or one of a few, in this movie, there are dozens of younger would-be Karolyns.

Right: Karolyn as the Little Match Girl.

Poster advertising the movie, *Hans Christian Anderson,* starring Danny Kaye.

Karolyn, as the Little Match Girl, looks at Danny Kaye (Hans Christian Anderson) as he sees Copenhagen for the first time.

Danny Kaye, playing Hans Christian Anderson, tells one of his fairy tales to an enthralled group of children.

Present Day

With her children grown, Karolyn now focuses her energy encouraging others who struggle with life's challenges. Karolyn has shared with me that she feels that there are balances in life. Even though she has experienced some rough times, in her words, "for me being Zuzu gives me the opportunity of meeting people and listening as they share their stories of surviving many of the hurdles of

The first reunion of the "It's a Wonderful Life" cast in 1993. From left: Carol Coombs Mueller (Janie), Jimmy Hawkins (Tommy), Karolyn (Zuzu), Todd Karns (Harry Bailey) and Virginia Patton Moss (Ruth Dakin Bailey).

life. I learned from helping my fellow man, making an effort to work with individuals one on one, whether it be taking a cancer patient to the doctor, helping with special needs children, or many other opportunities to give of myself. The love that I receive in return contributes to a continual healing process."

Always able to capture the camera at its best, Karolyn poses with her lovely smile.

She has lived life knowing loss and heartache, as well as love and adventure. Karolyn states strongly, "We have been given the ability to make choices. I have made the choice to always follow my dreams and not be afraid of change. One of my dreams was to live in the Pacific Northwest. As the millennium turned, after years in the Midwest, I moved to Seattle. Again, I start a new chapter. Life is an unending journey with a continuous unfolding story. We all can make it... a Wonderful Life."

It's a Wonderful Life is one of Capra's best films. It captures the spirit of the heart of America. Bedford Falls, the classic American small town, portrays the film as a wonderful place to live. George Bailey is an admirable man, sacrificing his own desires and becoming the classic "good guy" American character who always does the right thing. *It's a Wonderful Life* also is the ultimate feel-good movie. It has become a

Karolyn in New York, in 1990, spending the day with Jimmy Stewart, her movie father.

91

family tradition in many homes every Christmas time. Its sentiment reminds us of the best things about life, love, family and friends—that every person has a purpose in life.

With many of today's movies feeding an unending hunger with technology, special effects, death and deceit, it's no wonder that people look back to a time when things were simpler and family values were different. People long for those times, and the movies of those times reflect that era's messages.

One of Karolyn's favorite scenes in *It's a Wonderful Life* is when George is standing on the bridge. He realizes that what he values is nothing tangible. His family, his friends and the love they share are the important things. He puts his hands to his face and says, "I want to live again. I want to live again. Please, God, let me live again!" Then the snow resumes its gentle descent. It is at this moment that we know that he has returned to life and discovered its wonderful gift.

The adult Bailey kids preparing to ride in the 1993 Holiday Christmas Parade on the float for the Target Company. From left: Jimmy Hawkins (Tommy), Karolyn Grimes (Zuzu), Carol Coombs Mueller (Janie), and Larry Simms (Peter).

Born on the Fourth of July and representing the year 1940 for the photo of the Century sponsored by Kodak, Karolyn chats with the representative of July 4, 1900, Debby Marx of Belleair Bluffs, Florida.

Getting ready for the Detroit Thanksgiving Parade, Karolyn flashes a smile and a candy cane, 1995

An early morning radio interview with Jim Cates on Station WIBW in Topeka, Kansas.

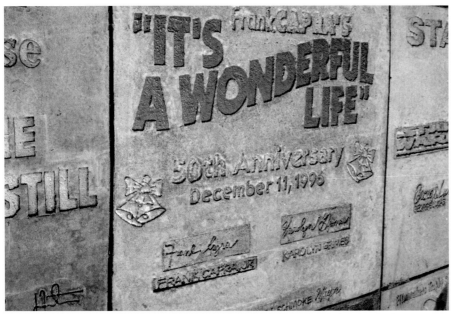

Nest to Frank Capra, Jr., Karolyn's signature is in the concrete in front of the Senator Theater in Baltimore commemorating the 50th Year anniversary of "It's a Wonderful Life."

Frank Capra, Jr., Karolyn and Chris Brunell appear at a fund-raiser for Hospice in Wilmington, North Carolina, 1999

5: AM, Karolyn starts her three hour radio satellite tour in 1998

Karolyn today

Karolyn shown breaking ground at a ceremony for a playground to be used by handicapped children in Florida

93

Today, Karolyn can be found at:
ZuZu
P.O. Box 145
Carnation, WA 98014

Or through the internet at:
www.zuzu.net